WORDS FOR THE HEART SERIES

Presents

MOMENTS FOR THOSE TIMES

FOR THOSE TIMES YOU NEED REASSURANCE THAT THE PEACE OF MIND, HEART AND SOUL ARE STILL AVAILABLE.

R. DARRYL ALLGOOD

MOMENTS FOR THOSE TIMES

2020 by R. Darryl Allgood

This is a work of fiction. Names, characters, businesses, places, events, locales, and incidents are either the products of the author's imagination or used in a fictitious manner. Any resemblance to actual persons, living or dead, or actual events is purely coincidental.

For questions or comments about this book, please contact us at the address below.

ISBN (978-1-7923-5152-5)

Printed in USA

Words For The Heart Series
Nichols, South Carolina 29581
843-540-8936
wordsforthehearts@gmail.com
www.abiblicalstartministries.com

This book is dedicated to the memory of our grandson, Carson Allgood.

<u>Preface</u>

In moments of confusion, heartache, discouragement or in some cases, even death, what do we do and where do we turn? Who can help in finding the solution? These questions have been asked each and every time one finds themselves in these situations. They leave one with emptiness, pain and sometimes hopeless feelings with no direction or path to recover. People will say, it gets better with time but in that period, what are we to do to help and assist in those painful moments?

In all of the authors situations in life, he has been able to pen words that will reach down to the deepest part of your heart and soul to reassure you of several things: (1) Your are not alone and (2) There is hope, love and understanding from oncs that havc already been there and experienced those same situations. There are so many blessings and comforts with all of the compliments of others in the past after reading these words.

Table of Contents

<u>Introduction</u>

Like many of you, I too, have had many ups and downs in life and asked myself the questions each and every time, What is the reason? Why has it happened to me and my family? What lessons and principles are meant for me to learn? The answers may come at a later date or even many years later but until then, I will push forward and not become as the stagnant water that sits on the side of the road gathering more dirt and debris that will turn into bitterness or harsh feelings.

People are always in search of answers simply because it is our nature. I too, wish we could put those questions into the microwave and place the timer on thirty-seconds but unfortunately, it's not possible. The following pages are designed to be an encouragement, inspiration and blessing in some small or large way in your pain, discouragement, hardships, broken hearts or maybe something else. I pray for only the goodness and blessings in your situations.

R. Darryl Allgood

1

The Fawn in the Fold

© 2012 R. Darryl Allgood

As the morning was breaking and the air was so fresh,

The body awakened from a long needed rest.

The deer and the fawn so innocent and free,

Now moving and grazing, for their appetites appease.

All of a sudden from very deep within,

Came howling, a wailing, like a screeching violin.

The dogs were now trailing, their scent now so fresh:

For the quest of a challenge like a huge college test.

The deer and fawn quickly jumped to beware;

The deer gave her life for her young she did bear.

Now the fawn continues to journey, its life to protect;

But the dogs keep coming for its life bound to wreck.

It leaps; it runs and dodges for a while,

It seems like forever and millions of miles.

God's love so tender, so rich, and so deep;

It is able to sustain, to protect, and to keep.

As the fawn has now traveled, so long and so hard,

He crosses the valley with his wounds and his scars.

The dogs, now so close and hot on its trail;

The fawn is so weary and ready to fail.

Then out from the heaven, where God stands and can see

He reaches the fawn and issues a decree.

It is I the Lord God, the creator of all.

The earth and the moon and the huge waterfalls

How His arms are so strong, so loving and true

The decree was His son, for me and for you

The dogs with their goal to destroy and to dismay

Must now turn and run, for their master to obey

Never be alarmed when times dark and so cold

Just trust in the master as the fawn in the fold.

2

<u>*Its Name*</u>

2017 R. Darryl Allgood

It begins so small and tiny, no way to see with eyes.

It moves and grows so slowly, no way to verify.

As the days and months go by, the years and decades too,

Its growth is not determined, its name, there is no clue.

Now times provide the questions; they are truly a vast supply.

What is this troublesome question, surely one can clarify?

The hearts and lives so touched, the tasks and jobs performed,

They climb each passing moment and fight throughout each storm.

You ask what we are talking, what do we describe today?

It seems the size of castles and delivers the sad decay.

We all have truly known, all touched and so advised.

We do the right things daily, so much to exercise.

There is a vast amount of time we truly see each day.

As they search and grasp the cells that cause this disarray.

We pray and ask the Lord that He will provide the answer.

This thing that touches so many, its name we know as Cancer.

3

<u>The Silence</u>

2017 R Darryl Allgood

The day with a shine and the night with a star

True peace with each moment so close yet so far

As it hovers the oceans, and it holds to the bays

Yet the Screams in the valleys as it reaches the waves

The canyons so deep and mountains so high

It is where it remains for we all should draw nigh

We search, and we look for this treasure divine

As the workers and labors in the deep gold mines

There are places and castles that we all like to dream.

Like the cabins and nature with the cold water streams

After all we have seen and all we have done

A day is not a day without the bright warm Sun.

Now slowly close your eyes and clear your heavy mind.

Forget all your thoughts of fear and unwind.

No matter the size of those great big giants,

This place is with calmness; it is called sweet Silence.

4

<u>The Road</u>

2018 by R. Darryl Allgood

A trail is rough and dusty, curves and winding ways.

Sometimes its long and heavy as it leads without dismay.

We travel along this way, by foot, by jeep or car.

Our purpose, our way, our goal, no matter how long, how far.

The trail it never stops, its travels are far and wide,

To reach that certain place, it is always our clearest guide.

So when you're tired and weary, without that certain sense,

You have that certain question, almost a dark suspense.

A trail seems dark and lonely, it seems to never end.

It now becomes my road though I didn't comprehend.

Now God is all around, don't fret or be dismayed.

He gave the road our path, His love will never fade.

No rocks, no dust or mud now on the smooth and narrow,

I can push and travel on as the star-speckled sparrow.

5

Then and Now

2020 R Darryl Allgood

Our Life and its actions, the growing as it comes,

Bring joys and the sadness, the tests, the fun.

Things go south, down a jagged winding road.

No way to understand, no way to unload.

The steps, the runs, the jumps and the falls

We are molded and shaped, with the crumbing of walls.

Our life takes the turns; its bends and the curves.

As if a burning flame, the scars with the nerves.

We try and push on forward, tomorrow with its hopes.

We cannot see thru darkness, all of the ships and the boats

Out from above and ascending on time

Gods provisions and needs arrive to the blind.

The honor, the love so destined to reply

As promised and given like one of a kind

Now I'm lifted, supported, cherished and adorned.

No words, no sounds can ever be scorned.

I look back then and compare to the now,

His grace and His mercy is the wonder of how.

6

Rain Before The Shine

2018 by R. Darryl Allgood

When it seems you've lost direction and cannot see His hand,

Your storm has blown you over, and you find it hard to stand.

As the thunder rolls so sharply, it seems the night is drear,

Your feet grow tired and weary, you can't hold back the tears.

No longer views of flowers as when in days of old,

As if your soul is frozen and the night is oh so cold.

The rain is strong and heavy, and darkness seems so vast.

It soon will be all over as the sun will break the cast.

We know the rain must come, and days like this will fall.

Our strength is only weak, that's why on Him we call.

He said the rain must come; all flowers are in His care.

Without the blessed showers, they truly will be bare.

So when you see the beauty of all the flowers below,

Rain is before the shine in order for us to grow.

7

Thunder

2018 by R. Darryl Allgood

As the thunder rolls so loud without a trace of sight

It travels along its way, no matter the dark or light.

Its deep and roaring sounds, get loud and deep inside

Not like the times of old, when playing at ocean tides.

We stop and pause a moment as we rush from here and there.

No time to sit and rest, no time for family prayer

Now the rain with all its winds, the drops, and heavy lights

Bring a sense of insecure, a dark and dreary fright.

The Thunder with all its power, its strength, and heavy sound

As if a huge explosion, an ignition or the terrible battleground

So when we think of thunder, the rain or all its winds

The storms of life will come, for this; we can depend.

For after every storm, every drop of rain that comes,

No matter how big it stands, We will not be overrun.

8

The Night

© 2012 by R. Darryl Allgood

As the sun sets on the mountains and the skies turn out the grey,

The silence fills the midnight as the stars come out to stay.

You can start to hear the crickets, as a peace begins to flow,

Wild game begins to sleep as the moon puts off a glow.

Calmness covers the lakes as the breeze begins to rest,

God's creatures are more relaxed as they settle within their nests.

Small children are ready for bed as they have washed and brush their hair,

All snuggled and tucked inside, as they rest without a care.

The darkness is for a reason, it has a certain goal,

Without the proper rest, our body would take a toll.

The dark comes just in time, as God turns out the light,

We fall and drift asleep as we are always in His sight.

So when at night you wonder, why the darkness falls,

What is the final reason, why does it even call?

God always has a purpose; He always has a plan,

It was He that made the world, not the hand of mortal man.

9

<u>*The Man We Call Dad*</u>

© 2012.R. Darryl Allgood

I look at my life and all that I have learned,

There is no doubt; it was what he had yearned.

The adding, subtracting, and all that relate,

Keeping in mind, there was no debate.

He tells of the times when life was so hard,

He served in the War, our country he did guard.

Home he did come, as a soldier and proud,

He fought for his country, as he spoke to the crowd.

Now forming and shaping was part of his life,

He was gifted and blessed as a finely tuned knife.

His hands so skilled, talented, and free,

Like the sails on a ship that is guided by the breeze.

His ability was unique, if already you do find,

He was the only one, God's amazing to design.

God's purpose, God's plan as only He knows,

To transform his talents and a family bestow.

Now the boys and the girls for his life did await,

To be fashioned and molded, like a huge wedding cake.

All detailed, precise, as one does with the brass,

He guided his family as the teacher in class.

Now my mind is so vivid, detailed, and clear,

For the one that we speak, to my heart is so dear.

He has flourished and prospered in the life he has known,

For his children and family, he truly has grown.

No greater a man, as I stand here so glad,

As the one I do speak, the Man We Call Dad

10

<u>The Answer Is On Its Way</u>

© 2012 R Darryl Allgood

As a child goes to his parent and seeks a small request,

He is sure he knows the answer; he has given his very best.

They pause for just a moment, a pause before reply.

The child is somewhat nervous, afraid of their deny.

His dad looks through his glasses, smiles and said ok.

The child was so excited; the answer came today.

The answer is on its way, God promised He would supply.

The answer is on its way; it comes from up on high.

So do not hang your head, just lift your load and pray.

For God is on the throne, the answer is on its way.

Have you ever prayed your prayer, just waiting for God to answer?

It seemed so long a night, but you know He was the master.

Did you pour your spirit out with each ounce of your strength?

Was it in the darkest night, no matter what the length?

Just follow God's direction, just follow the one divine.

He hears your every prayer; He said your prayers are mine.

The answer is on its way, God promised He would supply.

The answer is on its way; it comes from up on high.

So do not be tired and anxious, just lift your load and pray,

Just shout with great excitement; the answer could be today.

11

Conquered

2018 R Darryl Allgood

As a small and subtle voice, like a whisper of the wind,

Very silent and yet still as it sores and it spins.

A silence and a stillness as it calls to us, our name.

There's a peace, a delicate moment when life lives without the pain.

A life that has a purpose, an endeavor, and a goal,

Push forward and always onward as the black upon the coal.

Each step takes on a meaning, each day with new joys.

It's the memories of a child with the excitement of the noise.

Its senses and the voice are complete in all their ways,

Make the most of all your moments as the gull in the bays.

Reach to the inner part, down deep within your soul,

Pull forth the massive drive, cast out the inner cold.

Don't stop with deep emotion, don't linger at life's door.

You will never regret the day of the work and endless chores.

So when you think of victory, and the honor it does display,

Go back and remember then, the days and working ways.

12

It Only Takes A Moment

When it seems that you have traveled your last weary mile,

Your body is oh so tired and you want to rest awhile.

You glance for just one look to see if you are alone,

Then dial on heavens phone, you no longer want to roam.

You quickly get an answer, the voice is loud and clear,

There is no way to question; you lose all sense of fear.

You can hear the angels singing, a peace of love divine,

The bells are loudly ringing the perfect timely chime.

He speaks with love so tender; a voice of care so true,

It has to me my father, he said, "Child is that you?"

You finally dialed that number; you no longer want to wait,

You took the right road now, you see the golden gates.

It only takes a moment to make a phone call home,

It only takes a moment, are you tired of being alone?

He's always glad to hear, to talk or just be there,

It only takes a moment, your burden He wants to bear.

Don't ever be alarmed, frightened or just dismayed,

It only takes a moment; he turns your night to day.

13

<u>Life's Growth</u>

2019 R Darryl Allgood

I remember the time when young and unsure.

When the days were so many and the nights were so pure.

Life grew with each year as we learned so much more.

The chances, the joys with each new open door.

A glance at the fields with the waving of winds

The grass and the wheat would curve with the bends.

Birds soaring and diving for food on each day

When worries and questions at His feet they would lay.

The home and the warmth as we looked down the road,

Kept us safe and unharmed no matter the load.

America the beautiful; The land that we love,

The beauty and freedom as cherished like doves.

Now Years have grown my soul and my life

I have family and children from my dear precious wife.

The babies once young now grown and abroad

Creating and growing their families to applaud.

The wisdom and words from the older back then

When we were yet young, still close to the pen.

Work hard in the day and rest by the night

Your duties will come as you make it your flight.

Go quick and be strong with each day that He gives

Your love and acceptance, they need as you live.

14

If I Only Knew

2018 R Darryl Allgood

If I knew a love like this would come along my way

If I knew a love like this could be my song today

If I knew I would meet a snow white dove as you

I would be a happy man as honey and Winnie the pooh

If I could go to a place so warm and beautiful

If I could write a famous song and the greatest musical

If I could paint the mountain skies the bluest of the blue

It would not come close to you, for this I truly knew

I push through every hour; toward the end of every day

I push through every storm and make it all the way

As you stop and think of love; as you ask yourself the question

Does it make you jump and shout with the morn it does refreshen?

Don't stop and trade your days, don't quit and throw in the tools

Keep on the narrow road, the reward is better than jewels

Remember as you work, pressing on to the fullest measure

You shall find and secure a love, beyond the finest treasure.

15

A Solemn Vow

2019 R Darryl Allgood

It begins with a smile and how do you do

A gesture of kindness; their profile to view.

The work and efforts put forth to complete

A building and structure; our life set to meet

We push; we strive; longing the day

The one; the only, never to betray

A life filled with glee, happiness, and joy

It started this journey, set out to deploy.

The good; the bad; its days and the nights

For this journey of love has taken its flight

Now months and years have taken a growth

When we met; when we married and taking the oath

Our family and children, He blessed and bestowed

Never an angry moment, no matter what the load

We make it and strive for the day to rejoice

I love and adore you; I made you my choice.

16

Take One Step

The grandest old story of years gone by

Still holds to that power from up on the high.

Lives changed, made whole and turned all around

He takes broken homes and sends them Heaven bound. It

only takes His love, so real and unflawed

Regardless of the time, there is no facade.

Take one step towards the cross of Calvary

He'll do all the rest, it's called the victory.

Take one step toward the Savior today

You will never regret, He never turns away;

God's power stands tall, above all the rest

Just take one step and He will give you His best.

As you travel in this world and you see all that's tossed

Don't let Satan rob you, for they too, are the lost.

Not knowing their heavy burdens or all that they bear.

Their tears that are shed, nor the heartache that they wear.

Remember that day, when you first heard?

Your life was all broken, your spirit was stirred.

You took a step towards Jesus, you followed the path He lead

Your life He has now altered; just simply for being fed.

You grip that seat beside you, then run and hide your face

The Spirit has opened my door, simply for His wondrous

grace.

17

Babies Don't Quit

A small child, growing up in stages, has never known fear or being afraid as he attempts new things each day of his life. I can remember when my first child was taken to his grandparents at his crawling and slowly walking stage. He would hold to the coffee table and work his way around it, touching and even trying to pick up things he had never seen before. When he turned loose of the table and attempted to walk away, he would fall and roll over, but would get back on his knees and work his way back to the coffee table and try it again and again. He finally was able to walk away from the table with more stability and strength than he had before.

Now, he is in his early twenties and a senior in college. Years have passed since he was that small and I know, as a parent, we all can agree to similar stories as this. There is another area of these stories we tend to overlook. Our lives as young or older adults can be halted due to a trial or tragedy that has arrived in our path. We attempt to face it with strength, but with our strength and not God's.

We approach the table as the small child does and when we turn loose, we do well for a second or two, but we then tumble and fall down and begin to worry, fret and then realize, "Hey, let's try it again." This time, we attempt it with more caution and a better understanding of what is needed to make it work with more and added strength. This comes with time and practice, not forgetting patience and endurance. I like the old saying by Timex Watches, "They take a licking and keep on ticking." That philosophy can be adopted by each of us as well. The life we live will always have obstacles, bumps and even potholes, but that is ok and acceptable as long as we remember this one thought -- even though we fall, face a major crisis or some other event, we can get up, make up our mind as that child did and go full speed ahead. It's ok that we fall or stumble along the way; this is our learning process which, in return, will bring us wisdom. Therefore, we too should be strong like the babies that never quit.

18

Never Forgotten

2018 by R. Darryl Allgood

He was born in a little town, so small and off the map.

Not much for big productions, for this, there was a gap.

He grew so very slow, no fault to anyone.

All the kids would laugh and grin, for he, they'd overrun.

As time would pass by slow, it seemed so very long.

All others would run and play, grow tall and very strong.

The goals and huge ambitions that many seemed to feed,

He never quite understood though he never would concede.

Now the time has quickly vanished, and years have come and gone.

He has grown so very weary, vast surgeries he has drawn.

He would try to walk a line, keep strong without a doubt.

The desire to skip and run, the desire to jump and shout.

Like others now and then, we trip and may fall down,

Get up another time, brush off without a frown.

Never to be unheard, Never to be forgotten,

He is our only child, our love and dear begotten.

They are always in our heart; they are always in our prayers.
They are never, no never forgotten, no matter how much our
wear.

19

Don't Let Tomorrow Go

© 2012 R Darryl Allgood

The silence fills the midnight as snow falls to the ground.

Our love seems so exhausted as we struggle without a sound.

We say our love is real, no other can take our place.

The rose blooms in sunlight as we vanish without a trace.

We once could laugh and play, joke then kid around,

Now, all that's left of today are these pictures I just found.

Can you place yourself back then when we were so in love,

When we laid awake at night, admiring the stars above?

Don't let tomorrow go, don't say goodbye tonight.

I know it's not all gone; I want to make things right.

You're still my Cinderella, for me; you always shall.

Pick up the heavy phone and let your fingers dial.

Don't let tomorrow go, recall the nite we met.

I came to have a ball; I always dressed to deck.

I saw you sitting there with friends of yours I'm sure.

I knew you were the one, my love had reached a cure.

Now as we sit and ponder, recall the moments then,

Don't let tomorrow go, don't let it be the end.

20

<u>Gods Beauty</u>

© 2012 R Darryl Allgood

The Lilly of the valley, the bright and morning star

He is the great creator; though I am near or far.

The Mountains and the sunset, the colors of the skies;

When you think that no one loves you and you question,"Oh Lord

why?

Just take one glimpse of Calvary, the cross it will reveal;

There is no one, no other; His love is oh so real.

He's the rose of every morning, the star of every night;

The highest of every mountain and the brightest of every light.

Much deeper than any sea, far greater than any space;

God's beauty is far above any problem we ever face.

God's plan we often ponder and do not comprehend;

We go through many problems; our hearts He always mends.

We pray and search the scriptures; we look to Him for strength;

Our path has now been cleared, all done without a blink.

So when you feel no beauty, no care, no love or call;

Just look at all He's made; God's beauty is all in all.

21

Time

2017 R Darryl Allgood

When we stop and look back at the life we have lived

There is so much more we wished we could give

The up's and the down's and the choices that were made

Did we put forth our best in all that we gave?

Life seems so fast and driven by speed.

Was it out of control? Did we take time to heed?

God blessed us with family, children, and homes.

As we grew and were nourished in strengthening our bones

Hours turned to days; weeks then to years.

In all of our endeavors, with all of our careers

You asked me the question if we could go back and redo.

Would anything be different after a gigantic review?

Can we alter, can we change, can we rewind the tape?

Can we change our minds for our families to reshape?

Time is so real, vivid and clear.

Like a fine-tuned machine with all of its gears

God's design is so perfect with all of his ways.

Just view all of this, the world, He displays.

Life is a vapor, it's here and then it's gone.

But come to the early morn; he gives us the new dawn.

Cherish each moment and nurture your time.

Make sure it's your best, make sure it is prime.

22

Because Of Lee

I have run so long, with my guilt and my shame,

The hurt in my heart, I cannot explain.

No dream or purpose have ever I known,

My life, my family, and all that I own.

All wasted and gone, dwindled away,

Not knowing the answer is all I can say.

A knock at my door one dark gloomy morn,

A child appeared, clothes withered and worn.

With a smile of contentment, happy with glee,

He gave me a tract and said, "My name is Lee."

"Thank you," I said, as he went on his way,

He shouted, "He took it" on this one Christmas Day.

I pondered a moment and thought for a while,

"Maybe this is it" as I spoke out loud.

I decided to read it, what have I to lose,

Its better to read, rather sit here and snooze.

A plan so warming, so loving and kind,

I could not believe it was here all the time.

Transforming and wonderful it was all to me,

Simply because of a boy named Lee.

Years have passed since that wonderful day,

That little boy Lee has now passed away.

He yielded his life and obeyed a call,

Not knowing my life had reached a wall.

It is I now knocking from door to door,

I'm giving this plan to all rich and the poor.

So very grateful for the willingness, you see

For I would not be here had it not been for Lee.

23

Perfect Strength
© 2012 R Darryl Allgood

People say that they can make it; they rely upon their strength,

No need for Bible direction, they're strong though never weak.

But then a sudden crash, as life drops to the ground,

Thinking all is lost and over, pondering on heaven bound.

You say you're satisfied but thoughts of fear await,

And when you think of death, you ask "What is my fate?"

Oh real and perfect strength is always found with Him,

No worries about tomorrow, His light is never dim.

Just when I think its over, He always shows His face,

Giving man another day, filled with love and tender grace.

Now you think of all your friends, family members too,

And wonder how you can tell them, what Christ has done for you.

Just stop and count your blessings, name them one by one,

It surely will amaze them, what God has daily done.

Now strength, it is not purchased or requires a certain class,

Just simply come to Jesus, which is all the Savior asks.

Oh real and perfect strength, is always found with Him,

No worries about tomorrow, His light is never dim.

Just when I think its over, He always shows His face

Giving another day, filled with love and tender grace.

24

Love Fresh

2018 R Darryl Allgood

The day seemed like Heaven when I saw you afar.

My breath was amazed as it tore with ajar.

The birds with their voices as the choir from above,

Kept singing and singing as the beauty of the doves.

The clouds with their whiteness and the blue in the skies,

Kept me moving and panting as to you I drew nigh.

As the years go by slowly and I do truly mean.

My heart has been struck as the angel when a teen.

Troubles will come with tests and their signs.

We will travel together like the trees with the pine.

Never be hearkened, afraid or distressed,

For you are my one, unique and the best.

As the day now closes and comes to an end,

Gods goodness and blessings with each day He does send.

You and I are forever like the breeze with the wind.

As our family is created, for our family, we pin.

25

Give Your Heart

© 2012 R Darryl Allgood

No time for family values, no time to stop and pray

No time to say, "I love you" is now the American way.

Children are fighting their family members and death at every hand

Divorce is not the answer even though they say you can.

It seems your heart is broken, it hurts and aches inside

He tells you "Turn it over", this is what you'll truly find.

Just give your heart to Jesus, there is trust with me today

Just give your heart to Jesus, I will never, ever stray.

I have traveled the road you're on, I've been that way before

Just give your heart to Jesus, the end of pain and war.

Now battles will come and go, and valleys great and small

it will seem you're out of strength, the verge to tilt and fall.

When you feel that no one loves you and all have run away

He'll wrap His arms around you and say I'm here to stay.

God keeps you safe at night though dark and soar afraid

You will sleep through all the storms to find another day.

26

Our Pain

When your body is weak and feeble, giving

pain that feels so bad,

When your life seems all forgotten,

The thoughts are only sad.

When life's train comes rushing by you as it hurries upon its way,

It carries a load of purpose, just what we cannot say.

Be thankful as we travel, upon our weary road,

For soon, we will be standing at the place we will unload.

As we look beyond our life, at the river we all must cross,

Be thankful for the narrow path, for God we never lost.

So as you sit and ponder, you weigh your body's pain,

It really does not matter; Eternal life will be our gain.

27

Sufficient Grace

© 2012 R. Darryl Allgood

Elijah in the Bible was a man of great strength,

Everywhere he did travel, he spoke with great length.

He always pointing upward, lifting up God's dear name,

Jesus is the Savior; the reliever of your pain.

Great deeds and wondrous actions, works and miracles too,

All because of God's grace, a life was made anew.

Sufficient grace each morning, sufficient grace each night,

Everywhere that you travel, we are always in His sight.

Never a darkened moment, we are left along the side,

Sufficient grace each moment, sufficient grace abides.

Now David was a small one, not that big if you recall,

He faced the huge Goliath, and the giant took the fall.

So when you feel bewildered, walked and spat upon,

Just be another David; just trust the Holy one.

He holds the every star, the moon, the sun and space,

The wonder of it all with His Sufficient Grace.

Sufficient grace each morning, sufficient grace each night,

Everywhere that you travel, we are always in His sight.

Never a darkened moment, we are left along the side,

Sufficient grace each moment, sufficient grace abides.

28

His Touch

© 2012 R Darryl Allgood

A Man was on his journey to a place he'd never been;

He'd heard it's one of gladness, for you see there is no sin.

This man had never spoken, not even "how are you?"

People would ignore him, they knew not what to do.

He spent his life for others; always giving of himself

He never asked one thing, he knew how others felt.

Always very quiet, never speaking you could say

He finally met the master, oh what a wondrous day.

It only took His touch to make a blind man see

It only took His touch to save a soul like me.

Though sails are oh so torn and the skies are oh so dark

His touch is the one that mends a broken heart.

So release from that seat, your hands so tightly clutched

You will never, no never regret being touched by His touch.

This man has grown old and many he has led

To that cross on the hill, where they put down their beds.

Now crippled and aged in the body below

Not able to speak but humble I know.

Once able to stand with courage and strength

A witness for God, he surly was meek.

As he stepped into Heaven, he had so very much;

When asked what the secret, it was His very touch.

Starting A Family

As a child, he seeks to remember, all the things he wished he had,

He cannot recall a home, to me that seems so sad.

He seeks to feel a history, a longing to be a part,

A union that is tied together, it is the longing within his heart.

Many years have passed him by; he has grown into a man.

He wants to start a family, but knows not to begin.

The fear of all his childhood, the dark and dreary days,

It is almost like a ship at night, lingering in empty bays.

Just then, at the spur of a moment, a beam of light comes forth,

To direct the ship ashore, just turn and go due north.

This man has now a family, one he truly can adore,

He found the right foundation; it is God, the real and solid core.

30

Walking Alone No More

2020 R Darryl Allgood

She was walking along the road though dark and so afraid

Not sure of where to go as the sun began to fade

She travels in her mind, back when small and growing tall

Each time with a fight, the screaming and a brawl

Her voice began to quiver as she forced to make it out

The sound of wondrous music, for this, there was no doubt

She would sing that old song, "Theres joy within the camp"

Her steps would see a light, as if a huge and great lamp.

This would be her daily route for many years to come

As she studied and practiced music, to learn guitar strums

Days went to weeks, and weeks into the years

Her family had gone before, it brought so many tears.

Her life is now so tall, for years had come and gone

She is now a rising star from her youth and Bible drawn.

Now she sings with such gladness, joy and compassion

The fights, the screams and brawls, no longer within her fashion.

God is always by our side, no matter the road or chore

His strength is ever real as we Walk Alone No More.

In 2007 R. Darryl Allgood was in an accident that caused him to have cervical spine surgery which left him laid up for approximately seven months. With the inability to move his neck and shoulders for several months, he began writing poetry that lead to his first book, A Biblical Start To Solid Foundations in 2012. He stated,"The words seem to come so fast, I could not write fast enough." In this book, he wrote and explained how building anything in life should be built on a solid foundation just as the Bible talks about the foolish man building a house on the sand and the wise man building his upon the rock. Your foundation in life is very crucial and can either stand firm and withstand the storms of life or fall flat at the first sign of struggles or difficulty. He later began placing his poetry upon landscape scenery to emphasize and speak even louder regarding inspiration, encouragements and strength.

Darryl studied Bible at Baptist University, Hyles Anderson College and Trinity Theological Seminary, later to receive his

Bachelor of Arts degree. He is very much a positive influence to everyone he comes in contact and loves music along with solo singing. He has spent many years working in all facets of church ministry from preaching, counseling, running of bus routes, church visitation, the teaching of children and adults in Sunday school as well as senior care facilities.

He and his wife now reside in South Carolina on a horse ranch where they spend time caring for rescue animals as well as their chickens and goats. He spends a lot more time writing and has written his first novel "A Call To The Beginning" and a revision of his first christian book, "A Biblical Start To Solid Foundations" coming out in late 2020. He continues to speak and encourage every time possible.

www.ingramcontent.com/pod-product-compliance
Lightning Source LLC
Chambersburg PA
CBHW061039050726
47592CB00004B/1517